"This is poetry of motion and action. In each of Denise Sweet's poems we are urged by example to run, to search, to map and remap our lives and lands, to grin, to tease, to learn, to question, to protest, and to remember. Most of all, these poems ask us to sing and to listen for the singing of creation."

—Heid E. Erdrich, Editor of *New Poets of Native Nations*

"A great spirit infuses this major body of work from Denise Sweet. The poems in *Palominos Near Tuba City* are charms, songs and stories, cries and laments; their scope and breadth are resounding. They are not so much spoken by the poet as spoken through her, spoken not so much to or about us as for us."

—Bruce Taylor, author of *The Longest You've Lived Anywhere:*
New & Selected Poems, 2013

PALOMINOS
NEAR TUBA CITY

NEW & SELECTED POEMS BY
DENISE SWEET

HOLY COW! PRESS
DULUTH, MINNESOTA
2018

Cover painting by Camille LaCapa.
Author photograph by Kara Counard.
Book and cover design by Anton Khodakovsky.

Printed and bound in the United States of America.

First printing, Spring, 2018.

ISBN 978-09986010-4-5

10 9 8 7 6 5 4 3 2 1

Holy Cow! Press projects are funded in part by grant awards from the Anishinabe Fund of the Duluth-Superior Area Community Foundation, the Ben and Jeanne Overman Charitable Trust, the Elmer L. and Eleanor J. Andersen Foundation, the Cy and Paula DeCosse Fund of The Minneapolis Foundation, the Lenfestey Family Foundation, and by gifts from generous individual donors.

Holy Cow! Press books are distributed to the trade by Consortium Book Sales & Distribution, c/o Ingram Publisher Services, Inc., 210 American Drive, Jackson, TN 38301

For inquiries, please write to: HOLY COW! PRESS,
Post Office Box 3170, Mount Royal Station, Duluth, MN 55803
Visit *www.holycowpress.org*

ACKNOWLEDGMENTS

With profound respect and great honor, I recognize those who have been a source of strength, support and good humor for these poems. A healthy number thankfully, but most importantly I acknowledge—

The Hoocak Nation, especially former chair, Jon Greendeer for helping me remember the history of Red Banks;

The Oneida Nation, and especially, my beloved Oneida Book Club Ladies who taught me how to tell a proper story;

the intrepid travelers of Mundo Maya—David Coury, Christina Ortiz, McKenna Brown, David and Debra Galaty;

Delyssa Begay and her loving family at Rough Rock; those friends who have walked with me for the longest time: Frank and Inez Montano, Melonee Montano, Kimberley Blaeser, Paul DeMain, Tsyoshaaht Catarina Delgado, Cristina Danforth, Andy Connors, Ernie St. Germaine, Art Skenadore, Sue Daniels, Marj Stevens, Carol Elm, Barry Silesky, Patrick McKinnon;

Ray and Cindi at 4 Pines Ranch; my mother, Pat, and the memory of the sweetest girl, my sister, Carol;

my sons, Damon and Vaughn whose achievements far outshine my own up to this moment and beyond;

I acknowledge the promise of the future embodied in my grandchildren, Jasmine, Bazile, Sophia, and little Jose;

and lastly, I acknowledge Michael M., whose loving presence now lights my way. Beloved friends and family, I present these words to you.

Denise Sweet
Green Bay, WI
October 31, 2017

CONTENTS

AND IN THEIR MEMORY...

Walt Bresette, Ellen Kort, Nadine St. Louis,

Eddie Two Rivers, Jim Northrup

and

Michael Rodriguez, Diane DeFoe

GLOSSARY

Ajijaak: Crane.

Anishinaabe: (pronounced "*Ah-nish-shin-NAH-bay*") aka Ojibwa, Ojibwe, Chippewa, Anishinabek, etc. The third largest tribal nation in the U.S., tribal citizens reside within the boundaries of Minnesota, Wisconsin, North Dakota, South Dakota, and Michigan; in Rocky Boy, Montana, and in provinces of Canada (plural: "*Anishinaabeg*").

Anishinaabemowin: The language of the Anishinaabeg.

Chimookamon: Predominant culture. Non-Indian presence. Non-Indian People. (See *Megis Shell Prophecies—Anishinaabe Migration Accounts*.)

Hoocak: (aka "*Winnebago*"; pronounced, "*Ho-Chunk*"); the first sovereign nation of tribal citizens—a veritable empire—to inhabit the boundaries of the current state of Wisconsin.

Ikwe: Anishinaabemowin (Ojibwe) for "*woman.*"

Ogitchidaa: Ojibwe for "*warrior.*"

Ogitchidakwe: Ojibwe for "*woman warrior.*"

Wenebozho: Anishinaabe trickster figure. Also known as Nanapush, Manabozho, Coyote, among others.

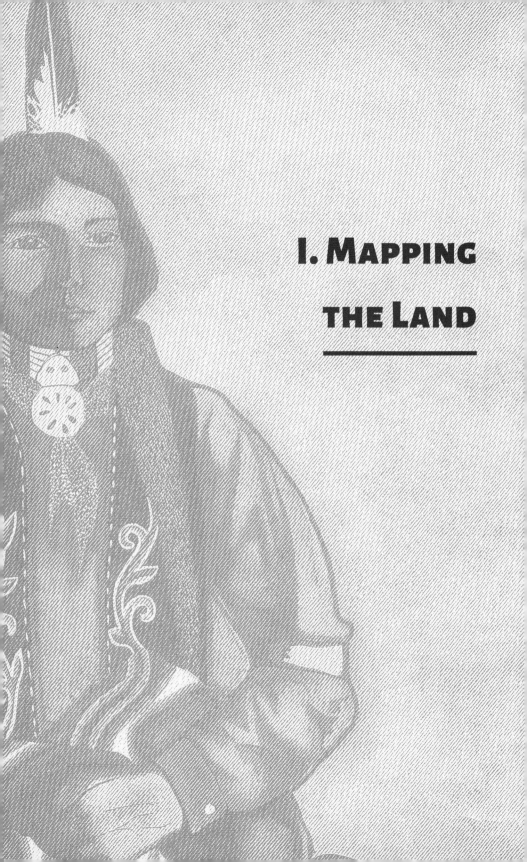

I. MAPPING THE LAND

MAPPING THE LAND

"Like the back of your hand," he said to me
with one eye a glaucoma gray marble
the brim of his hat shielding the good eye.
"You learn the land by feel"—each place
a name from memory, each stone
a fingerprint, while the winds rise from
the house of cedar.

At our feet, a five-pound coffee can
of spit and chew; the old man leans
and with remarkable aim deposits
the thin brown liquid without missing
a step; *"I never thought much
Of the running,"* the miles between
home and Tomah boarding school.

He has since teased me about the relays,
the long-distance marathons, the logic
of treadmills—who could explain this
to the old man? The sport of running
with no destination, no purpose, slogging
like wild-eyed sun dancers foolish
in the heat, snapping at gnats and no-see-ums
signifying sovereignty step-by-step
on two-lane highways, raising the dust
in unincorporated red-neck towns,
our fluorescent Nikes kicking up blacktop,
Ogitchidaa carrying an eagle staff like
an Olympian torch.

"Back then we packed the trail hard,
banking it for those who had no boots."
Schoolchildren, none older than ten
but wise in their running, a month
or two at home and then they would
be rounded up like calves into wagons,
Indian agents once again emptying
the villages of their children.

The older ones spoke no English and
slipped into their own shadows, kept
still in beds of bulrushes familiar and safe,
holding their breath as winter constellations
set compass, as northern lights danced
in a whir overhead, keeping track
of place and time.

"Home in a week by sunrise," he grinned.
"Every time! They'd never catch us!"
The old man looked straight ahead
and then at me. *"But I never finished*
the 7th grade, my girl." The sudden
twist of regret hung in the air
between us. I hardly knew what to say—

whether ignorance or stamina should
be his disgrace, whether I could've
found my way back home, lost
in the indecipherable space
of the Chimmokamaan;
would I run again and again

to return where my education would
unfold in seasons, within harvested stories?

Or, like some, would I have learned
the hard way; blinded by the light,
frozen by terror like a rabbit,
faking my death to stay alive?

COMPOSITION CLASS ON ADAMS STREET

Saturdays I'm at the cop shop
teaching English comp to
a group of officers.
My students talk around comp
of death investigations,
desk detail, and the myth
of donuts.

Some hint at how their wives
hate the flat-line moods
of their husbands.
They whisper to
themselves to
just do the job,
and once in awhile
a loser cop loses it
and shakes
the baby way
too much.

I'm not all that
surprised that I hear
about lives filled with edge
with hollow-point nerves
with trauma stories sealed
from the lips that sink
deep into the core
before we know it. One
officer finally mutters,

"That piece of shit will walk...
all of Seymour knows it."
We know it too.
Donuts crumble
in our hands.

Decades before this, I'd be
in bed while my parents
watched a crime drama
about clever cops and
trench-coat detectives
*There is a million stories
in the Naked City..."*
I had listened to that voice
once every week, pondering
crimes of passion, crimes
of vengeance or retribution
an abiding source of curiosity:
The many stories yet to hear of
in a town without its clothes.

Suddenly in Alabama (for J.J.)

We're peninsular, you and I,
jutting out into swollen waters
thick with roots and the wreckage
of race wars—a land mass
shaped for the loneliness that
simple hope can bring;

But the brave have their own
geography, following
a route not obvious or direct
compasses spin wildly
while off-road steering
moves boundaries past Selma
beyond L.A.
beyond Wounded Knee.

Whoever mapped your life
used no earthly legend
no codex rose in fire
for all the old and righteous
prophecies, we weren't
prepared for you

And as heroes do, you
moved among us, unearthing
whereabouts, dampening blazes
and steering hurricanes we hoped
never to encounter.
You did us good
Quoting Septima Clark

while children of ebony and light
sang by heart and
deep into the night,

> *"red and yellow, black and white,*
> *we are precious in his sight..."*

We must love the little children of the world.

Speaking Up in History Class

I'm reminded of the time
I took the Louisiana Purchase
personally in history class
and the teacher brought me
to the blackboard, made me
draw a straight line
between the ground
and the sky.

I was to stay within the lines
and pay attention to the margins.
I was to trace someone's sketchy
version of Western Civilization
by connecting the dots from
East to West, from here to
here then there

I thought this proves nothing.

Then she made me trace my hand
pointing out how crooked
lines are just like claws
and I grew weak from
the dark circles, from eyes
that looked like carbon sinkholes.

We learned by imitation, I said
and she whispered
"then watch me disappear."

At the Women's Studies Conference
(for Bea Medicine)

I remember that one time
when I was just sitting
next to Bea and
some powerful thing
I could feel, like when you feel
a branch above your head
is about to break if you're not still
so I was quiet and listened

while Bea listened and nudged me
while those behind us made
earth mother jokes and chattered
like magpies, while the women of
all red nations spoke to the audience
and, oh, I could hear that branch straining
about to break, just as I saw Ogemakwe.

Bea stood up and damn right, she told
those women behind us, boy,
she told them just what they didn't know
about women warriors like us, happy
to sing them into winding nightmares
right now, right here, if we have to
just so they'll shuddup.

And then they did, those women
behind us. Bea sat back down
and later I just had to ask
and she laughed at me 'cause

I wanted to learn that song
real bad.

No. No songs like that, Bea said.

We laughed at that one and ate our fries
at lunch. But didn't those wasichu shudder
right quick, Bea whispered.
I passed the ketchup then and
I was grinning, the both of us
just grinning.

MY MOTHER AND I HAD A DISCUSSION ONE DAY

And she said I was quite fortunate
to have two sons
and I said how was that?   And she said
with daughters, you worry for them—
birth control, child-rearing,
you worry for them, the threat of rape,
and then there is the wedding in expense.
I looked into her tired eyes
and clouded face and saw
that she was quite serious.   Yes, but, I said,
boys eat more.

My mother and I had a discussion one day
and she said why did they call it
Women's Music?
And I said because they sing it,
take from it, feel good and strong
when they walk away from it.
While we sit here this is going on.
Are you telling me, my mother said,
up until now I have been listening
and no women have been singing?
And I said that is right.
And she said that was ridiculous
and hummed a tune
Of her own.

My mother and I had a discussion one day
and she said why do you want to leave
this house? It is a fine house.

And I said I didn't think there was much of a market
for a nose wiper, a kitchen keeper,
And under the bed sweeper
And she said my smart mouth
would get me in a lot of trouble one day.
And I looked at her scarred knuckles
and quivering chin and realized
that I have spit in the face
of a thousand thousand women and
I wept with my mother.

INDIAN WAR

It's hard enough to make simple talk of this
watching turkey feathers and greasepaint grins
dance akimbo upon the TV screen
the painted quarter horses carrying
costumed braves, the rider screaming
as though on fire. I'm disgusted by

what I would like to say
the hurtful words I learned from punks.
None will fit neatly into the fatness of gratitude
you're expecting from your Indians,
the ones you honor at half-time.

The parallels to Stepin Fetchit escape you
though you know as well as I do
that the N word will never show up
on a football jersey.
Your eyes go blank when I tell you

our skin turned red only when it
was treated like bounty, human flesh
torn from muscle and bone
the trade worth less than beaver pelts.
You have no memory of this
and I cannot forget it.

I could say eagle headdresses and
catholic chalices, talk about
religious freedom and name
the Ghost Dancers shot down

in America's first Waco, I could admit
the hideous self-loathing that sweeps
through our children like smallpox

but it is no good: My throat is parched
my voice ragged, and I disgrace
my grandfather with all this
unnecessary begging.

On the prairie of justice and imagination
I go back to the Lakota Nation and
the tradition of restraint and male mockery.
Making war by making a point
where a warrior would steer
his swift horse directly towards
an enemy, close enough to
thwack his adam's apple, close
enough to smear feces
in his hair, close enough to
slap his cheek and ride away
in low-belly laughter sending
that soldier back to his troops
limping with shame.

I call out to the 500 nations
that reside on this continent,
those like me who want more than this
those who want to roll back
the AstroTurf like Wovoka described
to coax the yellow undergrowth
back into waves of prairie grass;
we'll watch the Goodyear Blimp

combust with grandeur over
Paha Sapa, listening for the thunders
to give the last 10-minute warning:
Time enough to learn about the end
of the world, and time enough
to finally learn of playing fair.

7-Year-Old, Taken Away in Handcuffs: A Found Poem

"In urban South Baltimore, 1 out of 5 children suffer from
Post-Traumatic Stress Disorder." Newscast, 2/04

He does not feel pain
like we do,
does not learn
from mistakes,
avoids touch.

He has witnessed
as a squatter
violent murders
in the building he
occupies with other
throwaways

At 7, he pulled out
a permanent tooth.
His options are: sell drugs,
do drugs, or die.

Neurological damage
from constant shock
and terror sticks to
the neurons like
flypaper; never able
to feel ever
forever.

THE LOST MAYA

At Panahachel, I sat in cathedrals,
lit candles to invoke the patron saint
of beggars, a statue poised to gaze from
within a wooden alcove, his eyes bearing
down on me in stone-cold indifference.

Light fell through stained glass as I gave
prayers a chance; *cofradias* swing tin cans
at each doorway, burning pendulums
of copal, while stiff planks beneath
my knees show years of anonymous penance.

As I leave for the *zocolo*, I hear the click and
low whistles of young boys sitting outside
on the cathedral steps; though my skin brown,
my nose Mayan, and I call myself indigena,
I bear an unearned pride that makes no sense here.

To them, I am the *gringa* who hides her privilege
like a birthmark; groomed, well-dressed, and not used
to the heat, I am the foreigner of complaint of El Norte;
I sit each day, sip expresso, asking for a photo
to touch *huipiles* aquamarine from Aititlan
Cortes, blood-red as the lava from Picayu.

I watch bone games of chance in the park central;
black candles, popping eggs, the glint of gold
in the smile of *Mishimon* amidst smoke and fire,
the chatter of daykeepers, the high sound of *kachikel*
dances on the edge of the world.

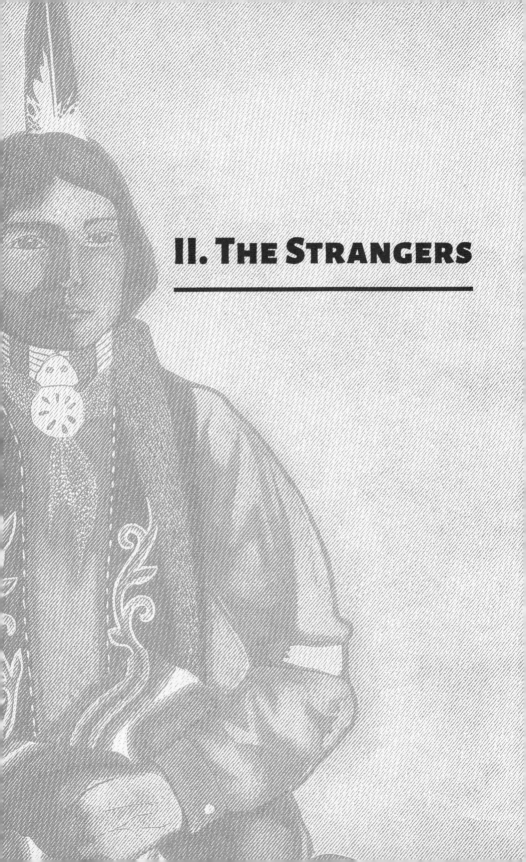

II. THE STRANGERS

Injun' Joe Remembers

"Did you think I'd forget? The Injun blood ain't in me for nothin."
Injun' Joe, *Adventures of Huckleberry Finn*, by Mark Twain

If I could make it rain I would
make it rain all over these hills

I'd ride that horizon, not through
valley or city, but between you and me

Little Ikwe, my faithful companion,
be the knock-bang posse behind me

We'll wear our famous smiles
and dance the dance of fire this time

Our hearts will rise on hope alone
we'll put words into words, watercolor

prairies painted tender and mute by the sun
forget the kimosabe who waves us back

I'll forget my lines again just for him
but the bloodlines will remember

and those songs we'll sing over and over
in the swirl and tumble of the canyon

until we are finally alive in this world.

"My One and Only:" Two-Step Blues

That's why when you go like that
you take the one heartbeat between us

When you go like that and do like that
the drums go like you like hawks go and do

They go up and up until one falls and one spins
When you go like that, the two hawks within

Ride near collide until they come in line with one
another and once again they're going like you go

A crow-hop, a two-step, a forty-nine for one
with one and once again they are one and do

And like you do, take the one heartbeat between them
and one falls and one spins like the drumbeat within

That's why when you go like you go and the drum goes
on until dawn, I cannot hear my heart and I cannot

Make a move. And you know it.

Wenebozho in Cream City

When the sun rises
he will be there
after he is asked
to leave. He does not
hear this, or this:
"No, you can't"
"It's never been done"
"Did you hear what I said?"

He pouts and never sleeps
and asks with a voice like
the Grand Canyon,
"Will you write poems about me?"
Then suddenly he is warm
emerald water, a tide coming
this close to your toes
and then skittering away.

A champion of concealment
an illusion of the landscape
and again with the hangdog look,
"It has never been easy for me,"
a whisper that drains like
ground glass, a child twisting
gently from your hand, then
gone before you know it.

2 AM Memory

You're awake at 2 am
and it's not the two lovers
quarreling outside, weaving
their way toward
an awkward bed.

It's not the thin and spindly
sound of the lone cricket
or the blistering heat
melting the paint off the walls.

What awakens at 2 am
are the racing thoughts,
the insufferable lists,
my arguments with the past

like peach stones
large and bitter
and impossible to resolve.
They're hard to negotiate
let alone swallow.

HOUSE OF DIAMONDS, HOUSE OF ICE

It is as it always is:
Casting off unneeded
      things to leave the rest
      until she can think
      of somewhere to go.

      Only this time
      she fears the sound
      of her own voice
      as she speaks of
      loud music,

      ugly falls and
      his beery glare as
      he drags his way
      into the house
      of diamonds.

That man whose
      eyes twinkle and
      fingers twitch says
      it'll be all right in
      a couple of days.

      And she can believe it
      it will be, mostly
      until a few bad dreams
      sweep and swerve
      again as the house of ice

surrounds her, as she
commits to memory
the details and her defense

and she can believe it
to be, mostly.

SHE MEANT EVERY WORD

That night, his famous smile worth nothing,
his voice an endless weight upon her days
too many to count—she meant it this time:

So he waits, his suitcases, setting hens
at the stairwell, his loose change, hat, and
keys thrown across the table the day before,
she watches out the window for his cab.
"Don't make this difficult" and he does
by reminding her of all the chances
he gave her to apologize, to change,
to sit, stay, to play dead.

He shoves against the door; expecting
he would stop and kick it down, she
circles the apartment and stops to stare
through the paper snowflakes on
the window. She turns to release
a one hundred-year-old shudder;
He had said *"I'm not giving up"*
and she thought, *Neither am I.*

But if she could say the words aloud,
and she took this more seriously,
she would see his fear, his helpless
tossing and turning through the night
and listen to him waste apologies
and his time. She washes her face then
and throws back a glass of wine
about to take her chances once again.

Alarming Light (Abbotabad, May 2, 2011)

That night the compound was warm and well-lit by
assuaging fires and the hearts of the women beside me,
women such as you, Amal Ahmed.
It was your young hands that clawed to stop them,
you who heard my cry of shock as I felt warm liquid
spring from my temple. It was you, not them,
taken from me by the uniformed others,
my blood-smeared face descending into shadow and hell
then, the sudden sound of orphans howling,
women pleading, soldiers scrambling,
and then the hour

of alarming light, at last, to which I drag myself
raging, fiery towers a storm of gray floating ash
so slow to settle in a gaping sky
and on ragged girders even a decade later.

I am of this and I am not;
women such as you, Amal Ahmed,
will lean against that heated rush,
will carry away a frenzy of revenge
and unlike those struck speechless,
you will whisper my name forever.

Amal Ahmed, the 5th wife of Osama Bin Laden
also named Amal Ahmed al-saran

Farmer Takes a Wife

The hard rains came end of February. Riverbanks melted into slur, new watermarks each morning, higher than the day before, just shy of flood stage. The long winter fever does not shake loose this time. Chills and night terrors sweep through the house until dawn. He cannot place the line once drawn from fever to delirium to insanity anymore, unable to decide whether to sharpen the axe or grease the brake lines of the family Buick. Who can blame him for not wanting to drag for days through acres of the black, musty soil, listening to Patsy Cline, chew packed hard in his lower lip? No amount of power will lift the heavy weight of crop failure this time from the White Earth prairie. Another favorite barn cat has drowned, lining like wet laundry to the woodpile. The baby rests on a damp mattress, waiting for the burial. Bread sits soggy in the pantry while his wife gnaws on the windowsill. The farmer has not moved from his chair for days, looking at the fields that held the seeds of everything he was to become, watching water slowly seep through the cracks. The Farmer's Almanac sits open to the charts of annual crop predictions while sprouted seeds ferment and bubble in the sludge, their yeasty odor everywhere.

ZEN AND WOMEN'S WAY OF PARKING

We know sooner than we think
when the vehicle we are driving
refuses to be herded into its stall.
We crank the wheel and ease our way
around and in and back and forth
and then back out and forward and in
again and then back and forth and
back and forth 'til we have neatly
and carefully negotiated a big thing
into a small space. It's all in the wrist
when we speak of power steering
or of our lover, for that matter. And yet

it is a maneuver that requires integration
of the body, mind and spirit; the contortive
efforts of the driver imitate Hatha Yoga
positions, as we are expected to see
front and behind, this side and that side
all at the same time. Be in the here and now
in the parking lot. Serenity is not far behind.
Neither is the Volvo parked in the next lane.

And how quickly we compute space, density,
width, length, and probability at that moment
we grind the gears from first to reverse
and back again; after careful deliberation,
the geniuses that we are, we arrive at the
parking nudge principle: Simply put, it is
a necessary and tender act to nudge the
vehicle to the front and back of us as we

locate the parameters of the space we are
to become. Oh, to be parked in a stall
of our own, but spiritually connected with
all that exists around us. Nirvana is achieved.

And the headlights are on.

Let them call us lady drivers, let them curse
and shake their fists at the *"battle-axe behind
the wheel"*—we'll give them no fast break,
no free ride; indeed we will not yield, even
though the sign insists. Oh sisters,
this is the right of way revolution. A woman's
way of parking is knowing and seeing
and feeling our way around this hard, flat
landscape we call parking space. We have finally
come to a place of which we surely belong.
We are at last in the driver's seat
and we laugh in the face of cruise control.

SENSIBLE SHOES

It's not the look
that turns me away
or the simple line
strict defining
way about them,
or that they gently
bend my arch
to meet a contour
proper, or even
the tiptoe quiet
they will provide
as I enter the room
unnoticed by other
shy and quiet soles.

I turn away from
the safe and sensible
shoe, the saddle or
the loafer, and harbor
a foolish longing for
the pump or the spike
Even now I lie awake
at night, dreaming
my flat feet lifting me
to reach another's lips
my tiny feet with
pointed toes or
perhaps a low slung
strapped seductive heel
in whorish red velvet.

It is odd to covet
the bound foot,

the treacherous totter
in black patent stilettos
toes that numb and stiffen
in the unwieldy glass slipper.
I will never dance with others
in my sensible shoes, gunmetal
gray, seven and a half,
slightly worn at the toe and heel.

SONG FOR DISCHARMING

*"Hear the voice of my song—it is my voice. I speak
to your naked heart."*—Chippewa Charming Song

Before this, I would not do or say what impulse
rushes in to say or do
what instinct burns within
I had learned to temper in
my clever sick
while stars unlocked at dawn
anonymous as the speed of light
my gray mornings began as nothing
freed of geography and stripped of
any source or consequence. I was,
as you may expect, a human parenthesis.
There is no simple way to say this:
Drift closer, Invisible One, swim within
these stream of catastrophic history
Yours? Mine? No, you decide. And then
come here one more time so that I may
numb like dark and desperate, so that I
may speak you name this final round
you might think an infinite black fog
waits to envelope me,
you might think I drink at the very edge
of you, cowering in shadows while hawks
hunt the open fields of my tiny wars
but little by little, like centipedes that
whirl and spin and sink into the scorching
sands of Sonora or like gulls over Madeline
that rise and stir and vanish

into the heat lightning of August
I will call you down and bring you into
that deathly coil, I will show you
each step and stair,
I will do nothing and yet
it will come to you in this way:

that sorcery that swallowed me will swallow
you too, at your desired stanza and
in a manner of your own making
While I shake the rattle of ferocity
moments before sunrise, while I burn
sage and sweetgrass, and you, my darling—
while I burn you like some ruined fetish
and sing over you, over and over,
like an almighty voice from the skies
it is in that fragile light that I will love you
It is in that awakening that I will love
myself too in this dry white drought
about to end, in this ghostly city of remember;
You will know this too
and never be able to say.

*"Madeline Island" (OJB: Moningwaunakanning)—one of the
21 islands that comprise the Apostle Island archipelago of Lake
Superior, Great Lakes region, North America.*

Veteran's Dance, 1995

—after Oklahoma City

During this round
I wanted to think of you
then, when each step
meant something
and you would
be out of
the mirrored building
and in front of me
dancing too
Instead I danced alone
under the stars and
the wild sadness
of Oklahoma City
spoors of light
burnish the newborn
darkness,
there is a blank moon
tonight,
and no one to sing to
This is the worst war
we've ever seen:
surrounded and unarmed,
shadows
unraveling everywhere.

III. ROUGH ROCK

PALOMINOS NEAR TUBA CITY

In the desert of burning dreams, of armadillo and centipede,
I would call this night pitch dark back home
I would watch for any star to pass into dream song

or point of light called planet to whirl and twist like
a tiny pinwheel swallowing me to its vanishing point.
Here under pewter sky with words out of breath

I chase poems down like wild mares into fenced corrals
I watch close calls with wisdom rear and kick
against the fences of good judgment.

I used to think the skies brought them home,
thundering hooves and swollen bellies, ready to spark
and fire the dry bony floor, sulphuric aroma real as rain.

But now, the horses of white lightning gallop toward me;
afraid of nothing, they rush with an eye for hesitation
ready to brush up against my heart with their horse madness.

Here, it is the rider standing in the wavering heat, erect
and indisputable as a lightning rod braced in the open.
I stand my ground and wait, ready to hold on for dear life.

RED DOGS IN THE HEAT

All day long in the name of commerce
and hospitality, the gates of Taos are
open to visitors.

Tourists move from table to table
speculating on rain and
the uptown prices in Santa Fe.

Vendors and their grandchildren stack CDs,
refold T-shirts, carefully touch displays
of coral, turquoise, obsidian and silver.

Tohono Oodham baskets and pots
from Acoma sit like roosting hens
in the scarlet heat of the Pueblo.

A man in khakis and a porkpie hat
stirs through a tray of fetishes
from Chinle; he raises a coral necklace

like a rattlesnake from its nest.
He asks, "Do you think this is real?"
His companion shrugs and in the absence

of mirrors, she touches her hair once.
Her eyes appear to whirl like tiny firecrackers
lit by the heat and the glare of silver.

"You don't know how fucking real
it can get here." We all look up;
I pretend to also look for the source of conjecture.

The vendors will only speak in Tewa and only
to their grandchildren, scooping beads
with long needles; no one speaks much

until suddenly the dogs—mixed bloods
of the Pueblo—raise issue in the center
of the market, until the scurry of dogs

divide the nervous crowd while older dogs
twist and torment themselves in the heat
aiming to keep turf at any cost.

Two Taoan grandfathers sit and chuckle
in their lawn chairs, sipping diet cokes
and jutting their chins toward the ruckus.

Finally a woman shakes her apron then a switch
in the direction of the disturbance, and
the dogs scatter in all directions.

The instigator snaps at his own shadow
and collapses in the shade of someone's porch.
He'll settle it later.

The dust waves away the sudden argument
until it is well out of sight, but not everyone
moves comfortably after this

and I feel strangely satisfied; someone asks
for a clean toilet, others for bottled water—
even better, someone asks for their website.

I head for the porch where the old dog pants,
pleased to know I really love rez dogs, the mean
heat in Taos Pueblo, and its sudden tectonic shifts.

Untitled (for Tony Mirabal, Taos Pueblo)

Tony molds micaceous clay
with slender hands then he calls
to me from his studio where I sit
outside on the patio of his cool
adobe home; I enter where
blue moths collect on the screen.
I'd managed to stay within the pueblo
after hours; it seemed innocent enough
easy enough though beneath my feet
white heat radiates even after dusk.

He packs a fire within the ground
and it will build for days
until a blue white
rises within the vessel;
any weakness or hairline crack
and the eccentric one will explode
angry by the reckless impatience
of the artist, with a passion
destroying the whole batch.
I can understand its anger.

I tell him I am a relative of runners
in the heat, runners of earth and fire;
I know, he grins, and then directs
my hand to polish the green clay
and each pot with smooth white
stones in slow circles on
the shoulders of each pot.
Art doesn't come easy, he whispers.

He still runs at dawn, carrying corn pollen
trailed by the dogs of the pueblo
on a path older than the buildings
built along the thin stream
flowing within the village. He runs
at dawn to keep from the tourists
or to test for cracks or tectonic weakness
in the foothills of the mesas.
You are running, man of clay,
of blue water, of volcanic fire

we are still running, you and I
we are still running.

ROUGH ROCK I

October has left us empty-handed
the slightest sound ricochets
against the mesa walls

a limb from a Joshua tree drops
suddenly and even a lift of leaves
in the wind can startle us

as we speak of Emory and
the accident, or as we sit in silence
grief has not yet left this room

I don't begin the mornings without
a disturbance now; feral dogs snarl
outside at the trading post, then

an old horse rubs his back
against the lodge in which I live.
You've gone in such an early season

Even the ravens, even the clouds
waver then move in the umber sky
to hide within the hills

cliffs like ominous red ships move
through the dust storms,
a familiar mirage in Rough Rock.

Now, he will hear the earth carry
our weight, sounds of descending stars
or the passage of blue sky into storm.

Messengers must know how to listen
for the soft-spoken word; the hawk waits
to guide them toward that last stem of light.

ROUGH ROCK II
(SPIDER WOMAN ROCK, CANYON DE CHELLY)

That rock's one way to describe you;
sand, stone, or the heavy burden of heat
does not stand in your way

while the winds erode the arroyos
and synchronize with dust tides in
the desert traveling like rivers on the moon

glyphs map the long-time familiar
paths for man and woman, and you
move with the cluster of Seven Sisters

working the land in the wine-dark night
carrying seeds of the men and women
to inhabit the legends we are to become

You are the medicine in the womanrain
of the Great Basin, the blue corn, the pollen
for the prayers that go unexplained

while armadillos lumber across the desert floor.

FOREIGN EXCHANGE:
WHO WE ARE, WHAT IS OURS

We were new in this skin
when 300 of us gathered
at an American university
watching from a distance
a deep, azure spring night

Brittle and driven, I read
my speech, and hardly
knew what I could say or
do, now that you belonged
finally alive in your bodies

You and I stand and wait
beautiful and dangerous
to the world, looking
directly into history, so
easy to lose our place

In a history we have not
written yet, you raise your
hands, looking directly at
me, expecting an answer
and like an angel's wings

They drop to your sides
as I fumble for new words
to old songs back when
our voices were strong
back when we used to sing

      we shall overcome,
      we shall overcome...

This has happened before
I whispered, all of it,
with grace and abundance
all of it, she said, *with grace*
and abundance.

Art Criticism: A Found Poem

With smooth ribs of Verde Chiesa
a sculptured woman
is cast in bronze
the marble base catches

light from above like
an aerial view of
small rivers on the moon.

The woman is held in balance
by anodized aluminum
with a title plaque
and a poem reads

 Stages of Womanhood

 Teac(her) then
 Train (her) or
 Tempt (her)

 Then
 Moth (er)
 Then
 Grandmoth (er)

A young girl whispers
to her friend
"Now what would you use that for?"

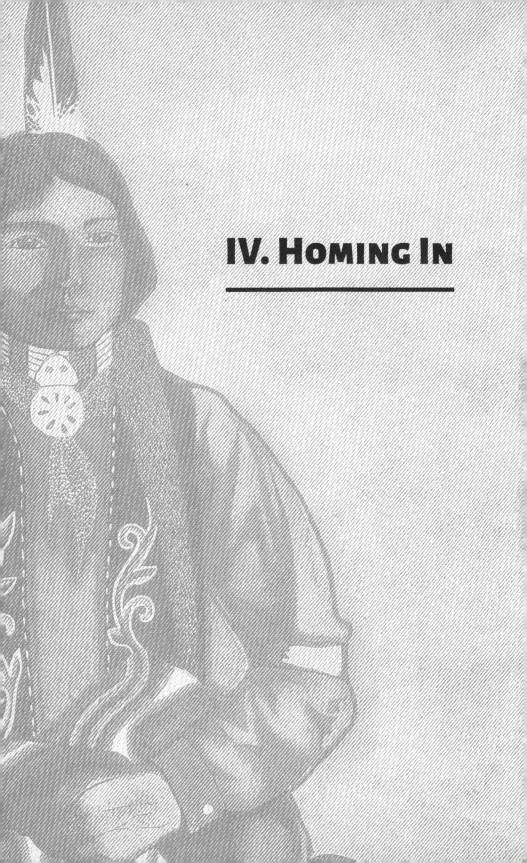

IV. HOMING IN

The Chill Factor: Earth Day 2017

It's an outer space near invisible
to the naked eye, distant
white-hot winds and
rhinestones from
the planets that
once sang—
stop.

And at the top of the world
sheets of ice tumble
into Arctic waters
while plankton
crazed with
hunger,
stop.

In their unexplained patterns
coastal seas make ready
For the 10,000 year
solar shudder
while we
stop

to finally wonder what daily strife
had ever brought us wisdom
in the end; or what earthly
sense our lives had
ever made so
we would
stop

...

The People of the Sea—At Red Banks
(For the Hoocak Nation)

I.   Beauty at its best is undisturbed in winter
the white wings of ice and snow
wrap its wings round this forest without
so much as a whisper.

The dry oak savannah fills and fills
without warning, without witness
and then one day we are buried
in our own mock amazement—
Where did all this snow come from?

As though drifts of snow and slates of ice
would not be here had we paid attention,
had we not slept through the howl of storm
or let go of the rope that tethers us to autumn.

II.   I wander through the wooded corridor of Red Banks
surrounded by silver maple, poplar, birch,
the slender red cedar stemming skyward,
left to plod and stammer through drifts
of snow with no tracks to follow, no maps
with arrows or stars, marking the spot
on which I stand—*You are here*

The sky is all I recognize. The star stories
and legends of naked-eye astronomers
Anishinaabe Adisokan begin to stir and whisper
and the names sway within the wind.
In my third season, I have finally learned
to be still. I have finally learned to wait.

III.   The People of the Thunders had gathered round
        the strangers at this inland shoreline

        the one spoke with great eloquence,
        with grand gesture in a splendid robe
        ornate with feather stitches, folds of satin
        those who could throw lightning with their hands
        and split the sky with such report, none could
        remember hearing such puny voices; such noise.

IV.   A red-tail hawk follows my curious wandering;
        beyond this wooded stretch is a highway and
        the distressed sound of 18-wheelers and SUVs
        sail through this moment towards an urgent other place

        wholly unaware of the slow searing sound of a hawk
        or the mincing steps of a white-tail deer before
        she leaves the wooded grove, before she races
        frantically, back and forth, and then
        across the highway into an open field
        or another quiet stand of trees.

        What moves, moves. A star story sweeping through
        the sky, a pure sound pouring over the heart of this
        wooded land; the origin of thunder here to be remembered.

SKY OPENS

—Nevers Dam, St. Croix River, July 2003

When all I want is dark
comfort, though it's
thin like the days
I walk into to
be able to
say who
I am

and where you are now,
like the star quilt I
hide under most
nights, where I
turn and pray
for sleep
and

all the incredible stars we see
have been there all along,
waiting to skid across
the sky, into the
canopy we
occupy
as we
go

to the river and count
them as they dive
and slide thru

the night
just as I
count
on

you to vanish from sight
just as I count on you now, some
stars are moving overhead
and we must think of
them as though no
one knows them
as we know
the stars
and like
you,

like relatives without names,
names without stories,
all I know is your
name and this:
A sky opens,
no one
has

discovered this night quite
like this, no one has
seen an open sky
ever before
like this
sky
or

open road, open river, or this dark
hidden night before this, or ever
made a discovery quite like
a new discovery like you
and I have, not one
like this one
till right
now.

STAND FOR SOMETHING

Birds do not fly—
they are carried
by the winds; and
as for fish? They
do not swim; they are
cradled by wave
upon wave. This
according to Feng Shui.

But, obvious to the Lakota
is *taku skan skan*—
What moves, moves—
Now, the guiding principle
along the Missouri and of
woceti sakowin;
reminding us to breath.

The Missouri now cradles
the Protectors of Water,
carrying them here
from the four directions
Is it reflex? Is it prayer?
Is it primal impulse
we had not counted on?

For months now, corporate
machines are at full throttle,
rifles are loaded, Morton County
poised and aiming, attack
dogs straining, choking
themselves, ready to lunge.

The Protectors are there
they are still there, they have
taken a stand to stand
for something, as rivers and
their tributaries carry and
connect us, as the winds
lift up over chaos to
a blue expanse, wind and water
stream and sky,
we are all tethered to the Protectors
we all drink from cupped hands
lift water to our faces at dawn.

We also stand for something
that which finally compels us
that essential thirst
for justice
for once and for all.

Where There Is Wind: Drum Dance

Let there be bells
Let there be bells of great heralding
Let there be bells in streets of long and low light
Let there be light for those streets long and low
Let there be harsh winters of great disaster
Let there be shelter for those without
Let there be snow-booted children,
smells of burning oak and stale sweat
Let there be winters of great disaster
whose drifts of rage and great fury
lift up over comfort and rest
Let there be rivers
Let there be rivers with no relent
Rivers that toss and swirl and glide
Let there be rivers of great hope
without rage and great fury
without torrents that sweeps away bodies
Let there be wind, and stone and sand
Let there be wind that moves us to lean and to stand
Let there be winds that surround us
Winds that compel us to continue
without wasting our lives.

We Learn to Use our Hands

Sitting before us like lumps
we want them severed
useless limbs without
repertoire or memory,
without impulse or reflex,

hands that would reach
into fire now seem stuck
on our bodies by accident
curled like dry roots, stiff
and atrophic like the wings
of dead crows: We'd remove
them ourselves if we could
but you see the dilemma.

Now, who will wring hands
with worry, who will drop
their palms in despair?
Whose hands can defend us
now? Who will do the scratching
as only we know how?
We cannot count on feet;
blistered at the toe and heel
they want no part of it.

The cold and cruel among you
suggest prayer while our fists
bang and knuckles spark and
the open palms lift skyward
and we learn the code

of the clenched hand: Paws
will dig and scrape for grubs
while hands in their inadequacy

suddenly swell and bloom as in
the pale pink rose of spring
no one let go, no one gave in
'til hands became hands again
firm in their common will
a sudden rainstorm builds
an applause and then
if by sound or roll call comes
an overwhelming show of hands.

THE RELIGION OF STONES

Without thinking, we drop two stones
into the precipice
one, courageous in its perilous descent
fires the path with shrill light
it goes beyond the unbodied
beyond the unnamed
falls away from its own reluctance
to fly in concentric circles
pooling inevitable waves
back to us.

The other arcs with
the velocity of confusion
veers and tangles
with the memory of ascent
like fever dreams
it shudders and flees
and moves through wind and rain
while a quiver of wings
suddenly appears
then suddenly its pewter body
a blood warm silhouette
heaving against
the gray crest of clouds.

LIVING WITHIN SONG

Those that kept us true
to course, those that held
our strength, that led us
to stand as people of this land
leaning into the fierce wind

of change without waver—
song so simple—
melody of Raven, of Coyote,
of waves that roar
and strain toward
the white sands.

Songs deep with memory,
echoing through the chambers
of every heart while marble halls
and statues collapse into dust.
The People understand place
and purpose.

They draw every breath
as though it was the first time
delivering songs of joy
to every being born
ever alive, ever to thrive
on this beloved earth.

UNTITLED (FOR THE SALT RUNNERS OF TIBET)

                                  hands rest on the table likes doves/while salt
dashed and sprinkled/ the polish of centuries of salt settled into glyph
patterns/aboriginal art of bone and rock scrubbed clean by wind and rain/
salt diminishing rock columns at Machu Picchu/salt licks square and red
and square and red/salt licks for cows/for deer/for yaks/licking finger to
finger/licking the salty sweat above the lip/swallowing the salt of labor/
the salt of griever's tears/salt of old sailors worth their weight in salt/timid
invisible salt whirling through water to settle at the bottom of the chalice/
smelling salts for the faint for the fearsome for the ill for the starving girls
of Trenton/salt into wounds salt into tears salt like deadly weight unto
our days/salt carried to streams from winter roads the gray and melting
salt/salt for the journey/salt for the pilgrimage salt as a sacrament, salt as
currency/weighed and measured and poured and tossed over the shoulder
and then from our eyes again water again this journey/salt distilled from
the sea, from mines of salt/soap/glaze/grit/each grain of salt a particulate
of time/salt we would die for/salt so close to ourselves we can taste it.

ALL THE ANIMALS CAME SINGING

Somewhere between nowhere and shadow
you held still and quiet, a quick slip and
you would totter over the edge of the world
taking with you ancient songs of love,
of devotion, of longevity; songs that celebrated
the simple elegance of living in balance.

So many whimpered in your absence;
the throat singers tried in vain to
call you back, other winged creatures
felt lost and cut off from the harmonious
crane song that once trumpeted
across the marshlands,
the width of riverbanks.

It was in our ignorance we fell silent.
Helpless, anxious to be of use,
we began to think of swamps and bogs
as eerie, ugly and useless
we drained those windigo wetlands
paved them over or planted crops
that floundered or refused to take root

Believe us, Aashigsug, we tried to fill
and give function to the emptied camps
of the whooping crane
or were we fumbling to fill that empty nest
in our hearts shaped by your absence?

We are told by the old-timers

that it is inborn in all beings alive
to return to the place of its beginning,
to rise and sweep with what strength
is left and begin that wondrous trek
towards home, no matter the distance
no matter how difficult the passage.

And so it is, Aashigsug. Shy, secretive
and cryptic in coloration, one day
you appeared in the bright mist.
As in your own emergence account
you stood before us, waiting for us
to send out a simple prayer, to properly
greet you by simply standing still.
You stood before us, elegant, erect,
majestic in form, a hooded shaman
from the farthest sky
out of range of the naked eye.

Through the bulrushes and overgrowth
of slender reeds, your mate steps forward
and with a slight but mutual bow and brief
address, you wander together, winding through
the wet marsh, springing onto a sandbar
and then suddenly a flawless lift into flight
punctuating the sky with prehistoric angles
some have never seen.

It has been more than one hundred years
since you have presented a clutch of chicks,
treasures of Necedah. Some indispensable
guiding spirit came into the heart of humankind

and coaxed you out of the shadows.
This joyous birth is a ripple away of the impossible
while you nudged your brood into thicker,
safer confines, we sang songs once again,
worshipping the ground you walk on
and all the animals came singing.

PUBLICATION CREDITS

Several poems in this collection were previously published in these journals, anthologies, and books:

Know By Heart: "2 AM Memory," "Sensible Shoes," "The Religion of Stones"

Days Of Obsidian, Days Of Grace: "My Mother and I Had a Discussion One Day," "Zen and Woman's Way Of Parking"

Traces In Blood, Bone and Stone: "Mapping the Land," "Indian War," "Palominos Near Tuba City"

Another Chicago Magazine: "We Learn to Use Our Hands"

Songs for Discharming: "Song for Discharming," "Veteran's Dance, 1995"

ABOUT THE AUTHOR

Denise Sweet is faculty emerita, having taught Humanistic Studies, Creative Writing, and First Nations Studies for the University of Wisconsin—Green Bay. She has performed in theater and film productions (both a full-length feature and various documentaries), and has given over 100 readings in North and Central America, Canada and Europe. Her books of poetry include *Know By Heart* (Rhiannon Press), *Songs for Discharming* (Greenfield Press, 1997), *Days of Obsidian, Days of Grace* (Poetry Harbor), and *Nitaawichige* (Poetry Harbor; the latter a four-author collection). In 1998, *Songs for Discharming* won both the Wisconsin Posner Award for Poetry, and the Diane Deborah Award, given by the North American Indigenous Writers Circle of the Americas. She is Anishinabe (White Earth).

Other distinctions: her poem, "Veteran's Dance: After Oklahoma City" took second place in Sante Fe Indian Market's 1st annual Poetry Competition. In 2006, the International Crane Foundation commissioned Sweet to author a poem for the organization, eventually titled, "All The Animals Came Singing." Additionally, her poem, "Constellations" is part of a permanent etched installation at the Midwest Express Center in Milwaukee, WI. In 1998, Sweet was one of five North American tribal writers sponsored by the U.S. Embassy to attend the 1st Annual World Congress on Indigenous Literature of the Americas held in Guatemala City, Guatemala. In 2004, Governor James Doyle appointed Sweet as Wisconsin's Poet Laureate (4-year term); the second laureate for the state.

Her works of poetry and fiction has appeared in numerous anthologies and literary journals such as *Cream City Review, Calyx, Akwekon, Sinister Wisdom, Yellow Medicine Review, Yakhiko la'tuse?* ("She Tells Us Stories"), *Another Chicago Magazine, Recreating The Enemy's Language* (ed. Joy Harjo), *Plainswoman, Returning The Gift* (ed. Joseph Bruchac), *Brave In The Face of Danger* (ed. Beth Brant), *Traces In Blood, Bone and Stone: Ojibwa Poetry, Stories Migrating Home* (ed. Kimberley Blaeser) and others.